# I Am a Carnival of Stars

# I Am a Carnival of Stars

ESSENTIAL WORDS FROM

**SONIA SANCHEZ**

ON LIFE, LOVE & RESISTANCE

BEACON PRESS, BOSTON

**BEACON PRESS**
**24 FARNSWORTH STREET**
**BOSTON, MASSACHUSETTS**
**WWW.BEACON.ORG**

Beacon Press books
are published under the auspices of
the Unitarian Universalist Association of Congregations.


Printed in China

29 28 27 26 8 7 6 5 4 3 2 1

This book is printed on acid-free paper that meets
the uncoated paper ANSI/NISO specifications for
permanence as revised in 1992.

Cover and text design by Carol Chu

*Library of Congress Cataloging-in-Publication Data is available for this title.*
ISBN: 978-0-8070-2525-3

The authorized representative in the EU for product safety
and compliance is Easy Access System Europe 16879218,
Mustamäe tee 50, 10621 Tallinn, Estonia:
http://beacon.org/eu-contact.

come windless invader

i am a carnival of

stars a poem of blood.

let me wear the day
well so when it reaches you
you will enjoy it.

what i need is traveling

minds talktouch kisses spittouch

you swimming upstream.

How to dance

in blood and

remain sane?

Your days still half-opened, crackle like
the fires to come. Outside. The earth.
Wind. Night. Unfold for you. Listen to
their sounds. They have sung me seasons
that never abandoned me.

then i began an awakening a flowering outside
the living dead became a wanderer of air
barking at the stars became a bride
bridegroom of change timeless black with hair
moist with kinks and morning dare
then i began to think me alive with form and history
then i made my former life an accessory.

but i am what i

am. woman. alone

amid all this noise.

would you please return
  my pulse? i need to tap my
  breathing once again.

i have told

you my name

so there is

tomorrow.

see me through

your own eyes

i am here.

(once upon an afternoon
i became still-life
i carried a balloon
and a long black knife.)

my husband sits
buddha like
watching me weave my
self among the sad
young men of my time.

your face like

summer lightning

gets caught in my voice

and i draw you up from

deep rivers

taste your face of a

thousand names

see you smile

a new season

hear your voice

a wild sea pausing in the wind.

the trees are laughing

at us. positioning their

leaves in morning smiles.

i gather up
each sound
you left behind
and stretch them
on our bed.
                    each nite
i breathe you
and become high.

how to erect respect in a country of men
where dollars pump their veins?
how to return from exile from swollen
tongues crisscrossing my frail domain?
how to learn to love me amid all the pain?
how to look into his eyes and be reborn
without blood and phlegm and thorn?

"Girl don't you know yet that you don't never give up on love? Don't you know you has in you the pulse of winds? The noise of dragonflies?"

we must learn to suckle life not

bombs and rhetoric

rising up in redwhiteandblue patriotism

"Let her be. She got a right to be different. She gonna stumble on herself one of these days. Just let the child be."

you ask me to run

naked in the streets with you

i am holding your pulse.

show me how

to be a revolutionary

overnight. wrap me in your

red orange rage

til i ripen in your black field.

i am moving in

air amazon woman bare

foot thunderbound bells.

what's wrong with being
freaky on stage you a stone
freak in yo own skin.

at least we up front
about this freakdom. at least
we let it all hang out.

For *we the people* will always be arriving
a ceremony of thunder
waking up the earth
opening our eyes to human
monuments.
  And it'll get better
  it'll get better
if *we the people* work, organize, resist,
come together for peace, racial, social
and sexual justice
  it'll get better
  it'll get better.

your hands

humming hurricanes

of beauty.

you, man, will you remember me when i die?

will you stare and stain my death and say

i saw her dancen among swallows

far from the world's obscenities?

you, man, will you remember and cry?

This earth is hard symmetry

This earth of feverish war

This earth inflamed with hate

Good morning, sex. How do you do?
Tell me how life's been treating you.
You say what? Sex is and sex ain't
sex wuz and sex wuzn't
sex should be and sex has been
on Times Square billboards
on television, in the movies,
in the lyrics dripping off pouting lips.
You say sex is in the drinks we drink
the laughs we laugh
the walk we walk
the smells we smell as we open
our eyes and legs and let the funk spread.
You say sex is dark basements
lights turned out, bodies turned on.
Sex is a breakfast table full of
leftover wine and smiles.

Sex is kinky & clean shaven
sex is straight & gay
sex is do it anyway.
Comes in twos and threes.
Comes on time. Late.
Sex is love. Unlove.
Comes with danger & beauty
Comes in clean and shadowy places.
Sex is life. Death. A gig.
Sometimes you need it in the
Morning. Afternoon. Evening.
Sometimes it satisfies; sometimes it don't
sometimes you feel it in yo' armpits
sometimes you feel it in the mind,
but ah, ahhh, when it comes
this sex, when it appears
buck naked or clothed,
when it comes Thelonious Monk–like jazzy,
when it comes hip hopping like the nite

ain't like no other nite; ya
know what time it is, what day
it is, what month it is, what year
it is. When it comes RIGHT, you
understand that sex is & sometimes it ain't
But when it is. . . .

do not speak to me of martyrdom
of men who die to be remembered
on some parish day.
i don't believe in dying
though i too shall die
and violets like castanets
will echo me.

And you told us: *the storm is rising against the privileged minority of the earth, from which there is no shelter in isolation or armament*

*and you told us: the storm will*

*not abate until a just distribution of the fruits of the earth enables men (and women) everywhere to live in dignity and human decency.*

my womb is a dance

of leaves sweating swift winds

i laugh with guitars.

Do we dance
death in a fast lane
of salsa

or minuet
death with an aristocrat's
pointed toe

do we ease
into death with
workingclass abandon

honey. It's too much you know.

*What?*

all this sex. It's getting so i can't concentrate.

*Where?*

at the office. at lunch. on the train. on planes.

all i want to do is sleep.

*Why?*

you know why. every place i go you're there.

if i cud ever write a
poem as beautiful as u
little 2/yr/old/brotha,
I wud laugh, jump, leap
up and touch the stars
cuz u be the poem i try for
each time i pick up a pen and paper.
u. and Morani and Mungu
be our blue/blk/stars that
will shine on our lives and
makes us finally BE.
if i cud ever write a poem as beautiful
as u, little 2/yr/old/brotha,
poetry wud go out of bizness.

love between us is
speech and breath. loving you is
a long river running.

"Is she a writer too, ma?"

"No, honey. She's a lady who has lived life instead of writing about it."

this day is not
real. the crowing of
the far-away
carillons ring
out direction
less. even you are
un real roasting
under a man
hattan sky
while passersby flap
their indecent tongues.
even i am un
real but i
am black and
thought to be
without meaning.

i see you blackboy

bent toward destruction watching

for death with tight eyes

this country might have
been a pio
neer land
once.
but. there ain't
no mo
indians blowing
custer's mind
with a different
image of america.
this country
might have
needed shoot /
outs / daily /
once.
but. there ain't
no mo real / white / all american
bad/guys.
just.
u & me.
blk/ and un/armed.
this country might have
been a pion
eer land. once.
and it still is.
check out
the falling
gun/shells on our blk/tomorrows.

your love was a port

of call where many ships docked

until morning came.

And I crept into my eyes. Alone with my daydreams of being woman.

autumn. a bonfire
of leaves. morning peels us toward
pomegranate festivals.
and in the evening i bring
you soup cooled by my laughter.

They were coming again, those words insistent as his hands had been, pounding inside me, demanding their time and place. I relaxed as my hands moved across the paper like one possessed.

It is essential that we always repeat:

we the people,

we the people,

we the people.

i've been a woman

with my legs stretched by the wind

rushing the day

thinking i heard your voice

while it was only the nite

moving over

making room for the dawn.

yeh.

billie.          if someone

had loved u like u

shud have been loved

ain't no tellin what

kinds of songs

u wud have swung

gainst this country's wite mind.

or what kinds of lyrics

wud have pushed us from

our blue / nites.

yeh.          billie.

if some blk / man

had reallee

made u feel

permanentlee warm.

ain't no tellen

where the jazz of yo/songs

wud have led us.

Her humming became the only sound in the park. Her voice moved across the bench like a mutilated child. And I cried. For myself. For this woman talkin' about love. For all the women who have ever stretched their bodies out anticipating civilization and finding ruins.

some

times i dream bout

u & me

runnen down

a street laughin.

me no older

u no younger

than we be.

don’t go. if you go

i won’t hear me. morning will

walk from me with life.

let me be your flute

fashioning laughter from this

bamboo wilderness.

ISHALLBECOMEACOLLECTOROFME.

AND PUT MEAT ON MY SOUL.

# QUOTE SOURCES

*Shake Loose My Skin: New and Selected Poems* (Beacon Press, 1999)

*Morning Haiku* (Beacon Press, 2010)

*Collected Poems* (Beacon Press, 2022)

*Homegirls & Handgrenades* (Beacon Press, 2023)

**A PROMINENT MEMBER OF THE BLACK ARTS MOVEMENT, WILSONIA BENITA DRIVER, WHO WE KNOW AS SONIA SANCHEZ**, was born September 9, 1934, in Birmingham, Alabama.[1] She is the daughter of Wilson Driver and Lena Jones Driver, who died in childbirth a year after Sonia was born, and she went to live with her paternal grandmother and other relatives for several years.[2] When her grandmother also died, Sonia developed a stutter, which made her more introverted but also turned her awareness even more toward language and the power of words.[3] Sonia would later overcome this speech impediment and attributed it as a special protective gift bestowed on her by her deceased grandmother.

At age nine, Sonia and her sister moved with their father to Harlem, where she attended public school, and in 1955, she received a bachelor of arts degree from Hunter College.[4] Sanchez then briefly attended

New York University and studied poetry under Louise Bogan. During this time she was involved in a Greenwich Village writers' workshop that attracted other Black Arts Movement figures such as Larry Neal, Amiri Baraka, and Haki R. Madhubuti.[5] Sonia went on to launch the Broadside Quartet with Madhubuti and other notable poets, including Nikki Giovanni and Etheridge Knight.[6]

Around this same period, Sonia married Albert Sanchez, with whom she had a daughter, Anita; the couple later divorced. Then, in the late 1960s, she married fellow poet Etheridge Knight and had two sons, Morani and Mungu.[7] They later divorced in the early 1970s.

Sonia became more politically active in the 1960s, first supporting the integrationist philosophy of the Congress of Racial Equality, then focusing more on Black heritage from a separatist perspective after embracing the ideas of Malcolm X.[8] Her earliest poetry collections, *Homecoming* (published in 1969) and *We a BaddDDD People* (published in 1970), feature uniquely Black perspectives and experimental forms of language, reflecting this point of view and voice.[9]

From 1966 Sanchez taught in various universities, pioneering San Francisco State University's Black Studies course in 1968 and securing a permanent position as resident poet and member of the English faculty at Temple University in 1975.[10] She became Temple's first Presidential Fellow and taught at the university until her retirement in 1999.[11]

Sonia has published numerous books of poetry and plays, and she has received numerous awards and honors, including the Dorothy and Lillian Gish Prize for lifetime achievement, the Ruth Lilly Poetry Prize, a Robert Frost Medal, a National Endowment for the Arts award, the Pennsylvania Governor's Award for Excellence in the Humanities, and the Anisfield-Wolf Book Award for Lifetime Achievement.[12]

Sonia Sanchez lives in Philadelphia.

# NOTES

1 National Women's History Museum, "Sonia Sanchez," https://www.womenshistory.org/education-resources/biographies/sonia-sanchez, accessed September 3, 2025.

2 Bobbi I. Booker, "Jazz Philadelphia's Hometown Heroes: Spotlight on Poet Sonia Sanchez," WTRI 90.1, April 9, 2021, https://www.wrti.org/arts-desk/2021-04-09/jazz-philadelphias-hometown-heroes-spotlight-on-poet-sonia-sanchez; Poets.org, "Sonia Sanchez," https://poets.org/poet/sonia-sanchez, accessed September 3, 2025.

3 Victor Fiorillo, "Sonia Sanchez Still Has Work to Do," *Philadelphia Magazine*, February 20, 2021, https://www.phillymag.com/news/2021/02/20/

sonia-sanchez-poetry/, accessed September 3, 2025; Anisfield-Wolf Book Awards, "Winners, 2019 Lifetime Achievement Sonia Sanchez," https://www.anisfield-wolf.org/winners/sonia-sanchez/, accessed September 3, 2025.

4 *Encyclopedia Brittanica,* "Sonia Sanchez," https://www.britannica.com/biography/Sonia-Sanchez, accessed September 3, 2025; Pennsylvania Center for the Book, "Sonia Sanchez," https://pabook.libraries.psu.edu/literary-cultural-heritage-map-pa/bios/sanchez__sonia, accessed September 3, 2025.

5 Pennsylvania Center for the Book, "Sonia Sanchez."

6 Anisfield-Wolf Book Awards, "Winners, 2019 Lifetime Achievement Sonia Sanchez."

7 Anisfield-Wolf Book Awards, "Winners, 2019 Lifetime Achievement Sonia Sanchez."

8 Poets.org, "Sonia Sanchez."

9 Pennsylvania Center for the Book, "Sonia Sanchez."

10 *Encyclopedia Brittanica,* "Sonia Sanchez"; Anisfield-Wolf Book Awards, "Winners, 2019 Lifetime Achievement Sonia Sanchez."

11 Anisfield-Wolf Book Awards, "Winners, 2019 Lifetime Achievement Sonia Sanchez."

12 Jeevika Virma, "For Poet Sonia Sanchez—at Age 87—There's More Work to Be Done," NPR, November 4, 2021, https://www.npr.org/2021/11/04/1052098986/sonia-sanchez-poet-profile; Poetry Foundation, "Sonia Sanchez," https://www.poetryfoundation.org/poets/sonia-sanchez, accessed September 3, 2025; Poets.org, "Sonia Sanchez"; Anisfield-Wolf Book Awards, "Winners, 2019 Lifetime Achievement Sonia Sanchez."